Canute The King
Still
I See With My Eyes Closed
The Voyage

two plays with music and two operas by Stan's Cafe

ISBN 978-1-913185-16-9

Published by Stan's Cafe
Birmingham, UK
2020

www.stanscafe.co.uk

Canute The King © Stan's Cafe 1993
Photos © James Yarker 1993
Still © James Yarker 1993
I See With My Eyes Closed © Stan's Cafe
The Voyage © Stan's Cafe 2012
Photos © Graeme Braidwood 2012
Publication © Stan's Cafe 2020

Contents:

Canute The King (stage version)	1
Canute The King (swimming pool version)	22
Credits	23
Still	24
I See With My Eyes Closed	38
Programme Notes	48
The Voyage	49
Credits	56

Canute The King
(stage version)

[The set is small, a simple draped fabric backcloth with a suspended window in its centre and a marble effect linoleum floor flooded with a few centimetres of water. A tea chest sits upstage left. There are two wooden school chairs on set, one has a cupboard door bolted to its back, this is the throne. There is some rubbish in the water on the floor]

[The King is unable to sleep. He looks out of the window then picks up a old fashion microphone. He broadcasts]

Tape: 1012 falling slowly, fine. Viking, Fair Isle, southerly 1, gusting 4, more than 20 miles, 1035 and falling, fine. Biscay, southerly 1, more than 20 miles, 1035 falling slowly, fine. And that ends the shipping forecast at 23:40 GMT.

Canute: Hello Everyone. "What a pickle we're all in," I know that's what you're thinking as you listen to me now, "what a pickle, how terrible everything has turned, how bleak it looks for us all in this beautiful land".

You ask "What of the Government? What are they doing? And that fellow Canute, what's he up to?"

You are right to be worried and to ask these questions and whilst I cannot speak directly for the government, I can answer for myself.

These last few months I have ben working on a scheme, a scheme which will turn this crisis around. There is still some work to be done on the fine details, but I have the answer to our problems.

I tell you all this now for it is an ambitious plan, it needs the support, not just of parliament, but more importantly of you, the brave subjects of this land, citizens of this crown. Together and with the grace of God we will turn the tide. So please, do not fret, all will be well.

From here in the palace the Queen and I wish you a peaceful sleep, good night to you all.

[The King searches the flooded stage with a torch. He finds a message in a jam jar. The Queen wakes up to see The King reading the first message, she too looks for bottles and jars]

King: What have you ever done for us?
Jonathan Shearwater, aged 14.
Queen: Good luck in your brave venture. Fond Regards, The Sultan of Bengal.
King: Your family have enjoyed privilege too long, let it sink without trace.

	Kate Longfellow, Romford.
Queen:	Thank you for your kind present, my thoughts are with you.
	The Crown Prince of Nepal
King:	Sink without trace. D.J. Young.

Queen:	Dear King Canute,
	We think you're great.
	With love from
	Sandra Dickerson and Family
	PS: keep up the good work.

Queen:	Doesn't the palace look lovely at this time of year.
King:	Yes it does, the staff do work so hard on it.
Queen:	We must remember to thank them somehow.
King:	Yes, we really must.
Queen:	Throw a party perhaps?
King:	Perhaps. Do you have much on today?
Queen:	No, for once my diary is completely free.
King:	I've got a couple of boxes but they won't take long.
Queen:	How marvellous, a whole day together.

King:	Is it really very late?
Queen:	I think it must be.
	[Pause] Shall I go shopping?
King:	Why not.
	[King acts as shopkeeper. Queen arrives.]
Queen:	Ready?
King:	Yes.
Queen:	Hello Mr. Simpson.
King:	Hello Mrs. Dickerson, what can I get you today?
Queen:	Let me think. I would like a tin of spam please.
King:	There you are. Anything else?
Queen:	Yes please, some toilet roll.
King:	Certainly, what colour?
Queen:	Blue please.
King:	Here you are. It's nice and soft.
Queen:	Oh good. Do you have any potatoes?
King:	Yes I do. How many would you like?
Queen:	Four please.
King:	There you are, that will be 50p please.
Queen:	Here. Do I get any change?
King	Of course, here you are.
Queen:	Thank you. Goodbye.
King:	Goodbye.

[The King takes a razor from his pocket and shaves in the water lapping round his feet. The Queen tidies up, she finds a glove puppet of herself]

King:	And here we hear the rock of buoys,
	All soothed in siren songs of dusk,
	Watch waves advance and waves retreat,
	And call it 'once again'.

King:	Why don't you sleep?
Queen:	I'm not tired.
King:	You're still playing with that thing again?
Queen:	Well? I like it.
King:	There's still no sign of the other one?
Queen:	No. It might still wash up.

King:	I don't know, I don't care. They're childish.
Queen:	I suppose so.

[She takes off the puppet. There is a moment of reflection and boredom. The Queen spots a new message but the King gets to it first.]

King:	My goodness look, here's one we missed, second post maybe. Shall I read it or would you like to?
Queen:	No, you read it, I already have.
King:	Really?
Queen:	Yes, quickly.
King:	Interesting?
Queen:	Well, moderately yes, moderately.
King:	Let's see... Presidential Palace etc. etc.. "My Dear Canute and Ael... Aelthruda," spelt wrongly.
Queen:	Again!
King:	"Thank you for" blah blah... *[reads silently]* Well I don't know, what do you think?
Queen:	About what?
King:	This letter.
Queen:	What bit in particular?
King:	All of it.
Queen:	Well, I only skimmed through.
King:	Well, some President is coming to dinner.
Queen:	What! When's this?
King:	Today, now, in a minute. He says here you invited him.
Queen:	I didn't invite him, at least not specifically, I don't think. One invites so many officially of course but not really, not to actually come and particularly not today.
King:	Well whatever, he's on his way.
Queen:	Let me see *[she looks at the note]*.
King:	What are we going to do about food and everything?
Queen:	Well this won't do. I can't do this... you can't just turn up, it isn't done!

King:	No, you can't just conjure up a gala dinner, kitchens don't work like that, these republic types don't understand.
Queen:	There isn't time even to approve a menu.
King:	There's no way he's getting dinner.
Queen:	Of course not, besides, I'm not very hungry.
King:	I'm not either.
Queen:	Not at all, in fact I'm full.
King:	A stupid time, the middle of the night!
Queen:	Well, we'll not see him, we'll pretend we're out...
King:	Out touring yes, absolutely!
Queen:	No, we won't do anything, we'll ignore it all.
King:	It's a bit rude but if we pretend not to have got the letter.
Queen:	Well look at it, a scrappy bit of paper, not a card, no gold border, this is impolite. You're supposed to send these months in advance on card and send it with a messenger.
King:	Eh?
Queen:	And a present. There wasn't a present was there?
King:	Sod diplomacy. What's that?

[The King starts picking up random items from the floor]

Queen:	There was no present with this was there?
King:	There usually is isn't there?
Queen:	Usually. *[Picking up an item from the floor]* What about this, is this it?
King:	No, no, that's not it. That was given to me by the Governor of Lithuania back in 1979.
Queen:	Ah, well it must be this then.
King:	Get your hands off that, that's sacred, you shouldn't touch that! It belongs in that glass case somewhere.
Queen:	Ah ha ha, now where did this come from then?
King:	I don't know. Ah that's it, that's it, it must be.
Queen:	No it's not.
King:	It is!
Queen:	It's not, it's yours!
King:	I don't recognise it.
Queen:	You got this in Boston in 1980.

King: I've never even been to Boston.
Queen: Yes you have, you went on your own in 1980. It's embossed on the back. "To King Canute, Best wishes from all the people of Boston, 1980. PS: Love To Queen Aelthruda".
King: Let me look at that!
Queen: Wait, wait a minute, this must be it.
King: No, the Philippines.
Queen: No, that's the Philippines, what's this?
King: Well Thailand then, Thailand. You remember, you wore that hat.
Queen: Yes, now you mention it, Thailand.
King: Hold on, what about this? This is new. Would he have sent a tomato?
Queen: Oh, I don't know, it seems a bit odd.
King: Well he's an odd fellow isn't he, do you remember that wooden thing?
Queen: Of course, did we ever decide what it was?
King: No, I don't think so. I think we lost it somewhere in the west wing.
Queen: Well if he is coming and he has sent a tomato he'll expect us to be eating it won't he.

King: Do you think so?
Queen: Yes!
King: Yes, yes I suppose so.
Queen: I'll ring down to the kitchens shall I?

[Here, as elsewhere, they realise their world is restricted to this rectangle of water - there is nowhere else to go.]

King: No, no I wouldn't bother them, and they're on holiday after all.
Queen: Of course. So are you going to prepare it?
King: Yes, I suppose so, um, how, how would you do it?
Queen: Well you've um... you've got to serve it with, well if you're not cooking it, which I presume you're not, then you've got to serve it with green bits, so it, you know, has red and green together and you've got to cut it into a coronet shape.
King: Of course, naturally, I remember now, a coronet shape, yes, most attractive. How the devil do they do that?

[The King starts cutting and The Queen starts waving her arms around]

Queen: It's this isn't it? Isn't he this?
King: I don't think so. That doesn't look like him, isn't he a foot thing?
Queen: Oh he's not... no no.. I'm sure it's this.
King: Hold on a minute.
Queen: Ouch! Yes that feels familiar, there's definitely some of this. Absolutely ruined my shoulder, it still twinges sometimes during croquet. I prefer to do that one but you can't can you?
King: I don't see why not, it's just the same.
Queen: No it means something completely different, its "get off my goats" or something. You don't want to greet the president with "get off my goats". He'll get all upset.
King: Yes, they're so picky, so easily insulted. I don't see how we're expected to remember all this prancing about. What about this, is this part of it?
Queen: No, that's Brunei I remember that, all those children doing that, it's not something you'd

	forget.
King:	Of course and that's Fiji,
K & Q:	Same trip.
Queen:	Let's work it through, we were in the car with the President, out of the airport, wiz, along the scenic route to the specially landscaped park, we got out and there were all those men, hundreds of them, looking very aggressive.
King:	I know, all covered in those big white circles and lines and what not, waving little flags.
Queen:	As always.
King:	Got the Union Flag all wrong as I remember.
Queen:	Anyway we're there expecting a bow or a march past or something when suddenly it's all this thing.
King:	That's it, that's it, you've got it, well done, yes. We can say hello to him at least!
Queen:	You know I don't think he'll come. He's supposed to be here already after all and he probably feels quite guilty for this protocol hash up.
King:	Then what are we going to do with dinner?
Queen:	Well it won't keep will it? And if he does come it's going to be a bit informal. I suggest we start and if he comes he can join in.
King:	Yes, that sounds reasonable, how about a table and everything?
Queen:	We had better do it properly.
King:	Right, that's good.

[They sit on chairs facing each other]

	You'd care for some of this?
Queen:	Why thank you so much, how kind.
King:	Salt? Pepper?
Queen:	Um, no thank you, I don't think so.
King:	Anything else?
Queen:	No, just as it comes will be delicious I'm sure.
King:	I'm sure you're right.

[They each eat their half tomato]

King:	Mm that was good.
Queen:	It was wasn't it.
King:	It was. You know sometimes... Sometimes I think...

	we're so...
K&Q:	Lucky.
King:	Exactly, very fortunate to be able to eat that tomato.
Queen:	I know.
King:	After all, how often do people get a chance to eat, just a tomato?
Queen:	The thing is you can get bored by abundance can't you?
King:	Exactly.
Queen:	And the strange thing is, if you can have everything you want, you're never able to choose what it is that you want.
King:	Exactly, it's a paradox, that's what you call the beast. A paradox that people just don't understand.
Queen:	A tomato isn't much and yet it's so much.
King:	A paradox, precisely, you never get a chance to have just a tomato.
Queen:	That's it, to get a tomato without the lettuce and cucumber and radishes and fresh salmon moose with dill dressing and creamed chilled garlic duchess-potato, well, you don't just get that chance do you?
King:	You know my father once said that when a normal man is faced with a choice between more than two things he goes to pieces and yet we have an infinity of choices every time we sit down for dinner.
	That's what people don't understand. You have to be bred to live with that scale of choice otherwise one wouldn't ever survive would one? You wouldn't end up eating anything, it's a miracle we don't starve.
Queen:	Who would have our job?
King:	I don't think I would.
Queen:	I think you're right.

[The King and Queen argue (improvised) it ends with]

King:	This isn't my fault you know!

Queen: Well it's certainly not mine!

Tape: 1012, falling slowly, fine. Mumbles, Cromarty: South Westerly 2 or 3, seven Miles, 1025, falling slowly, moderate to fair. St. Catherine's Point, German Bight, Malin Head: South Easterly backing Easterly, 4 or 5 rising later, 4 miles, 1025, falling slowly, rain or showers later. And that ends the shipping forecast at 23:40 GMT.

King: *[Over microphone]* Hello Everyone. "What went wrong?" I know that's what you are saying to yourselves. "What a disgraceful reception for a King, what a terrible waste of so sound a plan." You ask "What will protect us now? What will happen when the spring tides come?"

I share these concerns with you but we have faced worse dangers and together have always overcome them. It is my firm belief that, if you give me your support, this plan can still be realised and the waves kept from our doors.

I have spoken to my personal advisors and have decided that the barrier shall proceed. The first section shall be constructed here at the palace, by my own hands. When this section has proved a success all else will follow.

On this exciting note I must leave you. The Queen and I wish a goodnight to you all.

Queen: What are these doing on the floor?
What are these doing on the floor?

King: *[Picking up socks from the water, wringing them out and hanging them up on a chair]*
Right, you lot can go on here. Soon have you dried out. That's it chaps, how's that? A bit better eh?

Thought you were gonners there for a moment.
Rescued in the nick of time!
What a mess eh? What a terrible state. Well, has anyone got any ideas? Well? Don't be shy. Who's Minister for the Environment? You? Right any ideas? You haven't have you? Well you've never been comfortable there, so you're out. Reshuffle. Now who's Chancellor? You? No, you must be sport. So the chancellor is...

Good George, so strong of stitch and firm of weave,
so mute of hue yet warm of wool, what news?
How rates the odds twixt me and moon led tide?

(George): Alas the tide at one to none good King.
King: Are you sure? That's a bit steep, but do you think I can do it? *[He picks up and shakes socks]*
What about you? Or you? Anyone?
(All): No, good King.
King: You ladder in my sight, such darned
disloyalty does smell of treason and of cheese.
That this once loyal cabinet of socks
no longer boasts a single pair un-frayed
to stand with me 'gainst this most evil dawn.
(Sidney): I'm not scared.
King: Who was that? Ah, I should have guessed.
The odd one out as ever.
God bless you, hand wash you Sir Sidney Sock.
You're silk, the rest are viscose nylon mix.
So you're not scared then Sidney, is it because you're brave?
(Sidney): No.
King: Is it because you're stupid?
(Sidney): Yes.
King: I thought as much.
"Day sound is quashed in even-tide down drawn,
Well in the west the water sun is doused,
And silent from the sea a smother tide,
Is drawing tight around my neck and thine".

	What do you think of my poem Sidney?
	It's a love poem to win Aelthruda back again.
(Sidney):	Bar rotten fruit the only thing you'll win
	is prize for poetry that's shit.
King:	Thanks a lot.
(Sidney):	To take the Queen you need a rook that's sound,
	a knight that's brave, two bishops standing by,
	more pawns like me and poetry that's sent by God.
King:	This Castle rocks with every wave that thereon
	beats, and Church did leave me years ago,
	Of pawns I have but you, a worthless sock.
	I'm no brave leaping knight but broken King
	whose verse is sent from hell, or worse.
	Well what do you know? Bloody socks, who'd have them!
King:	So here I am looking out at the sea,
	we'll call it the sea for today.
	Down there are my gardens,
	my fine trees and hedges,
	for now I'll call it the sea.

[The Queen has moved over to the King with her puppet]

> I hear the waves as brown leaves blown by wind,
> see only black oil the scum and the floatings.
> I try to hold it all as I did in the past,
> but this time it's stronger than me.
>
> Time still passing, marked off on the marble,
> climbing the stairs.
> Sunday, I wonder the number of times we've been dreaming,
> Sunday, still no sign of the turning.

Queen:	I'm just nipping out to the shops alright?
Queen:	Hello, Mr. Simpson.
King:	Mrs. Dickerson, how nice to see you again.
Queen:	It's nice to be here.

King:	Shopping twice in one week? Is something wrong?
Queen:	No, my niece is staying, she has a healthy appetite.
King:	Good, that's nice for you. What can I sell you?
Queen:	A tin of Spam please.
King:	Anything else?
Queen:	No, not today thank you. And how much is that please?
King:	That's sixty p please.
Queen:	Is there any change?
King:	No.
Queen:	Oh.
King:	Mrs. Dickerson?
Queen:	Mr. Simpson?
King:	I was wondering, would you come to the pictures with me?
Queen:	No thank you. I must get back to my niece, we are having Spam fritters for tea.
King:	*[Finds another message]* "Help! I'm scared and I'm lonely".
Queen:	*[Writing a letter]* "There once was a lonely Princess, locked in a lonely country with a King who didn't care. She had given up on fairy tales and often cried. Then, one day, by a pool, a handsome man wiped away her tears. She loved him instantly and told him so, but he was from a foreign land, they had so much to say but shared no words. They married. He became a king and she became a queen. She was happier than she had ever been, until, one day she realised that now they could share words she'd forgotten all those things she had to say. But she knew he knew those things and loved her anyway." Still the waves are encroaching, but with no sign of the turning

we'll call now "the turning".

How did it come to rise like this?

We burn the maps of this complacent coastline,
cease to call it "jewel".
I read signs of storms in the skies,
can't check barometers falling.
Now all else is rising,
here comes "The Turning", I pray.

Some time, whilst we slept, the heavens signed a pact to align behind the pull of the grey faced moon.

Now I ask, "Why is it us standing where all these lines cross?"

Now I call "The Turning" in an ancient tongue. I call for a turning.

Tape: 1012, falling slowly, fine. Scilly, Dogger, Lundy: Easterly, violent gale 9, storm force 10 at times, 3 miles, 1010, falling, rain, hail expected later. Cape Wrath, South East Iceland, Finisterre: Westerly, gale 8 to violent gale 9, four miles, 1005, falling, heavy rain imminent. And that ends the shipping forecast at 23:40 GMT.

King: *[On tape. This speech has clearly been spliced together from fragments of other speeches in order to manipulate his message. '/' indicates a change of source]*
Good day. This is King Canute broadcasting from the palace. / Britain is in danger /our shores menaced from all sides. / We cannot let this beautiful land of ours sink beneath the waves. / I have heard tell of rumours/ "What?" you are saying to yourselves. / People have been

suggesting that my Royal / Powers are waning./
This is nonsense! / I was placed on the throne /with
the grace of God. I shall defend this land / in two
days time. When the spring tides come I / will /
turn the tide.

On this exciting note I must leave you. /
The Queen and I wish good night to you all.

*[The Queen is lying down in the water. The King pulls her out.
They embrace, eventually the King breaks the embrace. They
look uncomfortable with each other. The King goes to the
window]*

Queen: Is it nearly dawn?
King: It must be.
Queen: What's going to happen to us when you fail?
King: I don't know.
Queen: Do you care?
King: Of course I care. I care more than anything.
Queen: That isn't true is it.
King: It's not a lie.

Queen:	I know. I'd do the same, but I would tell you how I feel.
King:	What do you want me to say?
Queen:	Nothing that you don't want to.
King:	What are you doing?
Queen:	I'm making the bed.
King:	Don't. leave it! It's a throne not a bed.
Queen:	I need some sleep and so do you.
King:	Can't you leave this just once, for tonight, for me, please?

[There is a fight in the water].

King:	Hello Mrs. Dickerson.
Queen:	Go away.
King:	You left something in the shop… or rather, it's a present.
Queen:	What have you got there?
King:	It's a present.
Queen:	How much does it cost?
King:	Nothing, it's a present. I'll just put it down shall I?

[The throne and chair have been set up as a bench. On this bench The King puts his long wooden box. Opening it he reveals a fleet of silver foil boats with candles in their bows. He lights the candles and together they launch the boats out across the water].

King:	I name this ship Voice of Stars.
Queen:	I name this ship Fortune (favouring the brave).
King:	I name this ship Cheap But Sturdy.
Queen:	I name this ship Pure Of Heart.
King:	I name this ship Drifting Never Lost.
Queen:	I name this ship Red Sea Parting.
King	I name this ship Aelthruda (Smiling Now).
Queen:	I name this ship Simple Maths.
King:	I name this ship Faint Voice Just Heard.
Queen:	I name this ship Dream Of Valour.
King:	Let us name this ship The Long Voyage Home.

[The Queen sleeps, her head on the King's lap]

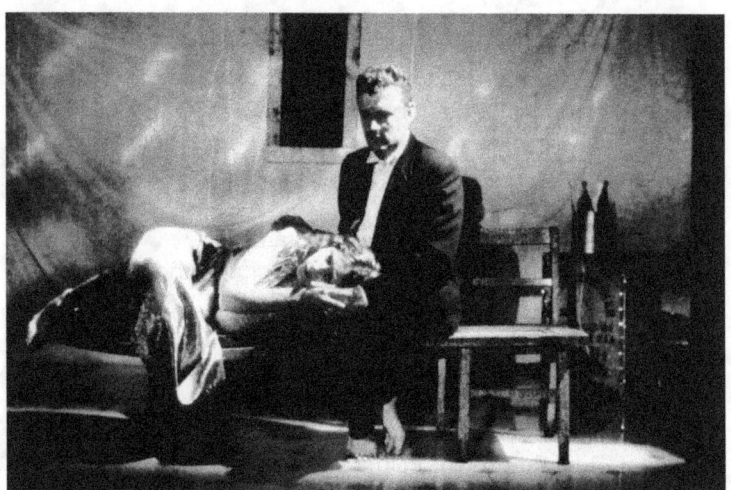

King: I took your hand and pulled you on.
I carried you, pulled you, dragged you forth,
past all you knew and outward still,
to where the blue-blood veins in flint-stone rock

now end.
To where the land now throbs and quakes in knowledge of its fate.

And now for now with nowhere else we'll call this bleak grace 'home', where carrion gulls scream "lay you down" and all fearful rocks dissolve into the sea.

King: *[On tape]* Um... Royal Palace Automatic: Easterly, probably backing northerly 1 or 2, completely dark but clear, 970 rising, spitting a bit by the looks of it and I don't know what it's like anywhere else, so that ends the weather, it's now um... 12:40.

England, bound in with the triumphant sea, whose rocky shore beats back the envious siege of watery Neptune, this fortress, this rocky throne of Kings, this sceptre isle, this earth of majesty, this demi-paradise this seat of um...

[Blows on microphone] Hello everyone, it's me, sorry I'm a bit late, I'm at the palace.

"What a curious fellow" you must be thinking. Well to be honest there's been a bit of a mix up. This turning the tide business, I don't think it's going to be feasible... You've got to believe me that I didn't say those things. I [taps mic] Hello.. Hello.. I hope you're still there.. I'm sorry that everything has been a bit of a hash up lately but it will all come right, honestly. This barrier thing, it's bound to work. Perhaps if some of you would like to pop round we could talk it through. The cabinet think it's a goer and.. oh sorry, must dash.

Night all, sweet dreams, God bless.

[Dawn dawns. The King sets up for turning the tide. The Queen wakes and helps him. The King, in his crown and cape is committed to the waves by the Queen]

Queen: Once sea now land now sea once more,
Once sea now land now sea once more,

And here we hear the rock of buoys
all soothed in siren songs of dusk
watch waves advance and waves retreat
and call it "once again".

Surrender to the rhythmic wash of surf,
we can but call it 'once again', for now,
and long for when the sudden shingle hush
will ebb through us again.
Deep in the ocean sky pinned carrion gulls call
echoes down on us
"lay down, lay down".

You look so beautiful down there,
You look so beautiful down there,

All clothed in waters of our past,
You look so small in need of rest.

History's seas are rising up,
embracing us to take us home.
"So down you lie and down you lie"
the shells all sing to take you in
and cradle you in finest sand of hour-glass quartz
and powder you in mica,
to drape you in a filigree silt of love and guilt
which washes from all the bedrock books of yore.

And now for old times and in place of all we call you 'King'
and hear the rock of buoys.

And now I call you "mine"
and call you "mine"
and call you "mine alone"
So now we long to rest,
to hear the sound of sleep.

And here we hear the rock of buoys
all soothed in siren songs of dusk
watch waves advance and waves retreat
and call it 'ever more'.

Once sea now land now sea once more
Once sea now land now sea once more

I say
"Maybe we are closer now than we have ever been before".

**Canute The King
(Swimming pool version)**

The touring stage version of Canute The King was adapted from a site specific performance staged around, on and under the water of Moseley Road Swimming Baths in Birmingham.

For this performance the audience sat on a public gallery around three sides of the pool.

This original pool version had less text and more visual material.

The photograph reproduced above is all that remains as a record of this event.

Canute The King Credits

Devised and performed by
Amanda Hadingue and Graeme Rose

Directed with text by James Yarker

Music by Richard Chew

Costume and set Stan's Cafe

Lighting on tour Stan's Cafe

In addition, for the swimming pool version

Lighting by Simon Gowan

Singing by Richard Chew and Cheryl Pickering
Harmonica by Joel Squires
Projections by Martin Crook with Ben Wheatley

With thanks to Sebastian Barnes, Collin Wallace
Dorothy Wilson, Mick Yates.

Both versions

Supported with funding from West Midlands Arts.

Still

Commissioned by Royal Opera House as part of its New Visions New Voices competition.

Music Richard Chew
Libretto James Yarker

Still was staged at the Royal College Of Music. It was not billed as a Stan's Cafe production and the action did not all follow the stage directions as laid out in this script.

Overture
[The conductor arrives without ceremony and blows an eight second blast on a bosun's whistle during which the house lights fade.

The overture begins low, a few bars in and the curtain slowly rises. With the rising of the curtain the Franklin folk song becomes audible. Its source is on-stage, apparently coming from the two televisions in whose flickering light two women are seen working on a conveyor belt along which anonymous tin cans pass continually. Their work is unfathomable, it barely requires their attention; they watch the televisions.

Both conveyor belt and workers are positioned above and behind the stage. The women appear to look down on the action which follows]

The Sailor's Dream
As homeward bound one night on the deep
Slung in my hammock I fell fast asleep.
I dreamed a dream which I thought was true
Concerning Franklin and his brave crew.

I thought as we neared to the Humber shore
I heard a female that did deplore;
She wept aloud and seemed to say;

'Alas, my Franklin is long away'.

[Arr. Joseph Faulkner 1878]

Woman 1: Do you ever feel like your shift has gone on forever, then look at the clock and find it's only just begun?
Woman 2: Always. Do you ever think about home and thank God you're here?
Woman 1: Always.

Act 1: Faking The Sea

[Lady Franklin's voice comes out of the blackness speaking text to a letter. As the lights come up we find her at a writing desk. As the subject matter grows more emotional she begins to sing]

Lady Franklin's Aria

Lady F: ...and further to this my Lord I would count it a small service if you could supply me with the detailed plans for the relief expedition. I require to know the number of ships which are to be sent, their names and the number of crew members involved. I am anxious to reassure myself that the Admiralty are sparing no expense in this matter. The coordinates of where the search is to be initiated are also a matter of concern to me. I have made my own calculations and wish to compare them with your own.

Lastly, I would be grateful Sir, if I could consult you on a more delicate matter, not in your position as Admiral but as a friend of my husband,

Is it possible that they have found the passage?
Could this be why we have heard nothing?
What hope that they will return to us, as myths from the East?
Is this too much to ask?

John are you listening for me?
Please, that you can't hear me now.

Ahh! John,
Why did you leave before I had a chance to speak, say all there was to say?
Why did I only think of the words as you sailed away,
think of them and whisper them to you over the widening sea?
By the time you think to speak, words are always too late.

I whisper to you now Johnny, for only in a whisper can you hear me,
"John my letters can't reach you now, as my tears didn't then, if this prayer will not help you then neither can I."

Stop me feeling God, hold me apart.
Don't let me think and take me away,
away with you John.
Take me away.

Why didn't you let me touch you?
Why wouldn't you kiss me?
Why did you shake my hand on the quay?

Come back to me as your old memory did.
Come back and displace this swift silent pain.
Come back because I don't know what to do.
I don't know how I've come to this
And without you there is nowhere left to go.

[As Lady Franklin releases the letter she has been writing it slowly rises in the air, it is the first of the stream which continue throughout the aria.

As the aria closes Hartnel, Braine and Torrington descend from their bunks. There is the clang of a bell. Lady Franklin lights a candle as the lights fade on her.]

Hartnel – Braine Shanty

Come the summer
Come the sun's glow
Here the thaw starts

Once rode a deep swell
Won round the good hope
Now she lies still, still

We'll last the night
Break the ice calm
Chart the passages
Soon we'll be home
Safe with honour
Rich and content.

[They have been singing in an attempt to ignore Torrington who is dying with lead in his system.]

Torrington – Lady Franklin Duet

[When Lady Franklin joins Torrington's singing the immediate thought is that they are singing to each other but they are not and are separated by time as well as space.]

Torrington	Lady Franklin
Can't keep a lamp lit	
Rage wracks the ship	
Fights in the galley	
Ice squeals our hull.	

Lead skin is soldered
On Iron and glass
Fetid air retching
Sounds of the black.

                                        Head is a blizzard, lessons beyond me,
                                        No one will take, this letter I write.

First time I've left you	Left long without you
And see how I'm failing	But love never doubted
Look at my hands mother	The search has begun John
See how I'm wasting.	May God make you strong.
Can't keep my mind straight	Can't keep my heart still
I've lost half my memory	The country is praying
See home in my fever	and ships out to rescue
And where is it now?	Oh where are you now?

[Braine and Hartnel interject refraining their shanty.]

Torrington There's fear in those eyes that ignore me
                 False notes in the song that won't hear me

                 No path to search for
                 And hostage to dark fates
                 Whose glory is sought here?
                 It's whose idle plan?

                 Dying for Franklin that book chewing pig
                 His pride and fame and reason to be
                 We're no longer mapping God's Jealous Land
                 A devil's own world we'll be pharaohs of ice.

                 All that I pray for
                 Is the rock of the swell.

Lady F: Feel safe with your brave heart ever in mind
Hearing your voice in moments of fear
Sent out ten search groups
And more to follow
Your glory now writ there
Your name will endure.

I've etched endless letters, my soul to yours
Sent by all means to usher you home
Bottles cast to the ocean, hope after hope
should all this fail they won't keep me away.

I pray you raise our flag
And sail back on the swell.

[Braine blows a bosun's whistle for silence]

The Conveyor Women's Minds Drift

[Deadpan but mildly amused, unconcerned]

- Woman 1: It's funny that, when your mind drifts but doesn't go anywhere.
- Woman 2: Like when you wake up and your arm's gone dead and cold and doesn't belong to you.
- Woman 1: Yes, exactly like that, only different, I suppose.
- Woman 2: You have to rub it to wake it up and it goes all tingly.
- Woman 1: Like when you're pissed and your mind drifts and doesn't go anywhere.
- Woman 2: We haven't had a good disco for ages.

Death Of Torrington

[Hartnel is reading over Torrington's body which Braine swings gently in a hammock faking the sea]

Hartnel: …what shall I cry? All flesh is grass and all the goodliness thereof is as the flower of the field. The

grass withereth, the flower fadeth; Because the
spirit of the Lord bloweth upon it: surely the
people is grass. The grass witherest, the flower
fadeth. But the word of our God shall stand forever.

[Setting of Isiah 35 sung by Hartnel, Braine and the conveyor-belt women.]

> Strengthen ye the weak hands
> And confirm the feeble knees
> Say to them that are of a fearful heart
> Be strong. Fear not' behold, your God will come with vengeance
> Even God with a recompense; he will come and save you.

[Once the singing has started Lady Franklin starts her reading, as if at a memorial service.]

Lady F: Strengthen ye the weak hands,
And confirm the feeble knees,
Say to them that are of a fearful heart,
Be strong. Fear not' behold, your God will come with vengeance.
Even God with a recompense;
he will come and save you.
Then the eyes of the blind shall be opened,
And ears of the deaf shall be unstopped.
Then shall the lame man leap as an hart,
And the tongue of the dumb sing;
For in the wilderness shall waters break out, and streams in the desert.
And the parched ground shall become a pool.
And the thirsty land springs of water;
In the habitation of dragons, where each lay,
Shall be grass with reeds and rushes.
And a highway shall be there, and a way,
And it shall be called The Way of Holiness;
The unclean shall not pass over it;

But it shall be for those: the wayfaring men,
Though fools shall not err therein.
No lion shall be there, nor any ravenous beast shall go up thereon.
It shall not be found there; but the redeemed shall walk there.
And the ransomed of the Lord shall return,
And come to Zion with songs and everlasting joy upon their heads;
They shall obtain joy and gladness.
And sorrow and sighing shall flee away.

[The singing/music finishes shortly after Lady Franklin has finished her reading]

[Torrington's body is left to come to rest in silence]

The Conveyor Women Find A Bulge

Woman 1: Have you noticed the bulge?
Woman 2: The bulge?
Woman 1: Yeah, the bulge.
Woman 2: Oh yeah.
Woman 1: What to you reckon?
Woman 2: Reckon it's nothing
Woman 1: How long have they been coming through like that?
Woman 2: A week, maybe more.
Woman 1: What do you reckon?
Woman 2: Gasses most likely.
Woman 1: Is that good or bad?
Woman 2: At a guess I'd say neither good nor bad, just different.
Woman 1: So, shall we tell someone?

Act 2: Discovery

[An Arctic island with three black coffins standing stark on the bleak white landscape, a helicopter noise, radio text, a whoop and three scientists in bright parkas charge onto the stage. They are wildly excited by the surroundings, yet soon get down to work. Tracy is a photographer, Brian the archaeologist who initiates the setting up of a grid of coloured tape, it is a wild knot of tape, by no means regular. The sailors when they are discovered are inside the coffins. They are the same stuffed dummies that are used in Act 3 with the exception that the faces are much more realistic and life-like in Act 2.]

Brian:	Tracy
Tracy:	Yeah
Brian:	Harry J
Harry J:	Yeah
Brian:	Are you ready?
T & HJ:	Yeah
Brian:	Right, let's survey
All:	Yeah
Brian:	Alpha Base Survey Commencing
Tracy	1 Sight from the south
Brian	We want a grid
Harry J	Ten by ten
Brian	Ten by ten
Tracy	2 through eight different angles
Brian	Keep them tight
Harry J:	Looking good
Tracy	Light reading great
Brian	Accuracy is all
Tracy	Brian freeze!
Brian	Cheese
Harry J	E1
Tracy	and B4
Brian	A5
Harry J	Marl flints
Tracy	Harry J Freeze!
Harry J	Ice Cream

Brian	No tea breaks here
Tracy	F stop 8
Brian	H9 footprint
Harry J	Iron Oxide Trace
Tracy	30 – 40 Zoom
Brian	Size 10G
Harry J	Wood fragment
Tracy	Coke can
Brian	Harry J, what size?
Harry J	Bagged, I'm 10G
Tracy	Idiot
Harry J	What?
Brian	Take more care
Harry J	Polar Bear
Tracy	Where?
Harry J	It's gone.
Tracy	Oh yea?
Brian	10.50
Harry J	It was there honest!
Tracy	Like hell! Roll 4 loaded
Brian	Wait, what's this?
Harry J	Visibility 3 miles
Brian	Tracy A4
Tracy	Coming
Brian	Analysis
Harry J	Hold it
Tracy	Got it
Brian	Analysis
Harry J	Bone
Tracy	Rotate it
Brian	Yes bone
Harry J	Age?
Tracy	Rotate
Brian	100
Harry J	Far more
Tracy	Rotate
Brian	Eskimo shit
Harry J	H2 a hankie
Tracy	Transparencies

Brian	Come on
Harry J	That's mine as well
Tracy	Fuji 200
Brian	There, here, somewhere
Harry J	What's this?
Tracy	What's what?
Brian	What's that?
Harry J	Black wood
Tracy	Ignore him
Harry J	It's true
Brian	You know, I think it's them.
Harry J	Picks
Tracy	Pictures
Brian	Shovels
Harry J	Crow bars
Tracy	Shots
Brian	Get it out
Harry J	That's it
Tracy	It's there
Brian	I've got it
Harry J	Have you got it?
Tracy	I've got it
All	Wow!
Brian	Well open it up then
Harry J	Right
Brian	Well?
Harry J	Right
Tracy	No
Brian	Well?
Harry J	How?
Brian	Hot water
Harry J	Coffee?
Tracy	No
Brian	That'll do
Harry J	How's that?
Brian	What?
Harry J	This
Brian	That's fine

Tracy	No
Brian	And here we have?
B & HJ	Wow!
Brian	Gently
Harry J	Easy
Brian	Put him down
Tracy	No
Brian	There's more
Harry J	There must be
Brian	Here
Harry J	Here
Brian	No here
Harry J	That's it!
Brian	Picks
Harry J	Pictures
Brian	Shovels
Harry J	Crow bars
Brian	Shots
Harry J	Get it out, that's it
Brian	It's there
Harry J	I've got it, have you got it?
Brian	It's there, I've got it
Harry J	Wow, Wow!
Brian	Wow!
Harry J	We'll open it up then
Brian	Right well, right well
Harry J	How?
Brian	Hot water, coffee
Harry J	That'll do, how's that?
Brian	What this?
Harry J	That's fine
Brian	And here we have?
Harry J	Wow!
Brian	Wow!
Harry J	Gently, easy, put him down
Brian	There's more, there must be, Here, here, no here that's it Picks pictures, shovels crow bars Shots, get it out, that's it

| | It's there, I've got it, have you?
Got it, it's there, I've got it
Wow wow wow we'll open it up then
Right well, right well how?
Hot water, coffee, that'll do. How's that?
What this? That's fine and here we have?
Wow, gently easy put him down. |
| Tracy | No! |

[All three of the scientists are now hunched over their equivalent sailors, Brian and Harry J are making gestures towards scientific investigations. Furtive glances and nervous smiles are exchanges when they catch each other's eyes.

As the sailors are discovered Lady Franklin brings on and unwraps a brown paper parcel. It contains the flag she gave to John before his expedition. She is shattered, she sings.]

The Flag

Lady F: No
This is it
That flag
His flag
Our flag back with me
His shroud
The frayed end of my hope, gone.

And here the world ends
No movement, no more
The distancing has started.

This is it, that flag, his flag, our flag back with me
I cannot end now.

No passage, no pass
I do not know where I am.

I have never been here before.

The Conveyor Women Feel Sad

Woman 1: It suddenly feels sad in here
Woman 2: Oh I don't know, I've just thought of a joke, do you want to hear it?
Woman 1: No thanks
Woman 2: Oh, okay. Save it maybe?
Woman 1: Yeah save it.
Woman 2: For later.

Harry J: I don't know much about this archaeology thing but, well I know you're something special. Over 100 years old and so well preserved. You've still got all your own teeth, your own hair. That look in your eye, your skin looks perfect, if we thawed you out you'd be soft to the touch.

Brian: You've a long way to go yet boy but you've got potential, real potential. Sure you could do the lecture circuit, the odd text book, no problem. You could do that right now, but that's academic stuff, anyone could get you that, Harry J could get you that, and it's peanuts! What you need is someone with vision and ideas, someone to take you into the big time. I've invested a lot in you boy, and you know why? Because I think you've got it.

Listen, I can bring you back to life. How's that for a career move? Think about it, back from the dead!

Tracy: So you're a media star now precious, they'll all want a piece of you. They'll say "The coolest hot property of the year" and you'll never rest again.

Harry J: I can't believe this has happened to me, that we've found you like this, it's like something out of National Geographic. It's incredible.

Tracy: You're going to see our discoveries and progress,

what you were aspiring to. You're going to meet the Twentieth Century, like it or not.

Harry J You've got so much to tell. I'm not very good at this kind of thing, asking personal questions and everything. I'm a geographer you see, a physical geographer, that's physical rocks and weather, not physical physical, you know. Surely you can tell us about your life, your job, what you ate, how you felt?

I feel all mixed up inside. I don't know what to say, ahh! Well "what's a nice guy like you doing in a grave like this!" Ha, well, who knows... umm.

Brian: You'll be an instant celebrity, the first person brought back from the grave; the oldest person alive; the youngest ever centenarian; you'll have the World Record for holding your breath. You'll be huge.

It'll all be a bit strange and confusing, but I'll be your manager. I'll sort everything out for you: photoshoots; interviews; chat shows. I'll teach you microphone technique and how to smile. I'll help you with the difficult questions, they'll want to interview me as well.

Why bother with chat shows? Can you dance? Sing? Do magic? I'll teach you, it's easy, we could do anything. We could make films!

Tracy: There is a way to keep from all this, to shelter away, if you trust me.
I'll hide you from their prying eyes, keep cameras from your face.
I'll save your flesh from knives and keep you tight. They'll never find you out.

> Keep me from thinking too long of this place
> and I'll hold you safe and still.

Harry J: And the folk back home, they'll never believe us. We'll show them the photos, but... The Institute, they'll love you, they really will. There was this guy from the ice in Siberia, but that was Russia – kind of awkward. And the guy from the peat in Ireland. They went insane about him and he was just a mess. And you, you're perfect. They'll flip. There's a professor down in Alberta, you're just his type, I know it. I tell you, if I could take you into The Institute, you know, that'd be the proudest day of my life.

Tracy: They'll never find us and never ask more of us. We'll close all the doors, windows and curtains. We'll let no light in, pull the plug on the phone, we'll be under the stairs you and me.

Harry J: Maybe it's not so far fetched, maybe. I don't know, maybe I'm too shy about these things. Maybe I should just try it, do it. Yeah, what the hell, it's all for the sake of science. Ever fancied a trip to Ottawa?

Brian: We'll be invited out by Presidents, Kings and Queens, and Sheikhs and... We're going to make history.

Harry J: That's it,

HJ & B: you're coming with me.

Tracy: We won't speak or smile or cry.
You're coming with me.

The Conveyor Women Discuss Fate

Woman 2: Do you know where this is all going?
　　　　　What happens to them all?
Woman 1: They all get eaten in the end.
Woman 2: Really!
Woman 1: I'd say so.
Woman 2: Is that a happy end or a sad end?
Woman 1: I'd say neither happy nor sad, just normal.
Woman 2: Oh.
Woman 1: What does it matter, they're just cans after all.

Act 3: Naming The Mirror Ball Heavens

[A mirror-ball descends gently from the flies as a mournful saxophone echoes round the theatre.

The ball reflects slow revolving galaxies and the scientists shuffle on with their bonfire-guy sailors. It is the last exhausted, hung-over dance of a wild, wild party. The floor is covered with litter of all kinds but mostly old cans, crisp papers, used streamers, balloons, fast food containers and Saturday night trash. Tracy slumps to the floor with her sailor. Brian still can't quite believe his high hopes have crashed. Harry J is broken up with lost love, he sometimes just about sings. They speak very quietly to their unconvincing sailor friends.]

The Conveyor Women Think About Ends

Woman 2: Is this the end?
Woman 1: Nearly.

The Ends

Brian:　　　This is it buddy, welcome to the big time.
Harry J:　　Yeah, we had good times, didn't we?
Brian:　　　It's 23:29, let's see you Rock and Roll.
Harry J:　　You know, I really thought "this is it".

	Thought you were made for me.
Brian:	Say, how do you like modern times? Huh?
	For the viewers sunshine – what's two times two?
B & HJ:	Now she lies still.
Harry:	Yeah good times didn't we?
Brian:	Come on Bud, let's see you rock and roll.
Harry:	We could've faced the dawn together.
B & HJ:	Now we lie…
Brian:	Just for me sunshine… what's two times two?
Harry:	You know I really thought…
Brian:	You're a sad, crap shit fuck.

Harry: "This is it"

Brian: It's 23:29.

Harry: Toronto and the sun's setting.

[Throughout the scene Lady Franklin has been walking very slowly firstly across to upstage centre then forward to downstage centre. At the end of their text the scientists quietly breathe in and out through their microphones making the sounds of waves on a beach. Lady Franklin stops and stands, slowly looking at the lights reflected from the mirror ball moving round the auditorium. Then, with great conviction and intensity she sings]

Lady F: I name this star mine
         I name this fear blue
         I call this hope you
         I call this heaven ours
         This sound I name STILL

[The wave sounds stop with the word 'Still' on an intake of breath, leaving the last wave hanging unbroken.

The curtain drops very slowly in silence as Lady Franklin's unopened letters fall like snowflakes from the flies]

I See With My Eyes Closed

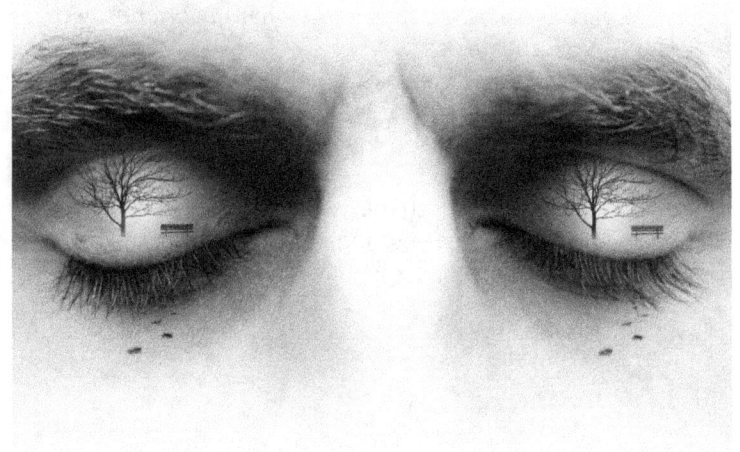

[Birmingham Contemporary Music Group are on stage. They tune up. The Conductor comes on and takes his applause. A couple come hurrying in to take their seats in the centre on the front row. The Conductor gives them a withering look before turning to start the piece]

First Movement

[*Just before the end of this movement the latecomers stir. We do not hear their spoken voices but their thoughts, voiced by other actors, are heard over the public address system*]

N: [*A satisfied exhale*] This is great.

Second Movement

N: [*Stands, adjusts himself*] I'll just sort myself out here, get comfortable.
S: [*Looking at N*] What's he doing? Sit down!
N: [*Sits*]

Woodwind Passage

N: I wonder if she's cross with me for being late?
Ooh this is that music from that film isn't it ... slow motion ... time lapse .... cars, commuters ....Philip Glass .... what's it bloody called? .... Forget it ... don't ruin it.
I wasn't actually late – just didn't have time for a drink ... not a great start to my treat I suppose.

Brass Passage

S: *[Shrugs neck]* I'm so tense. My shoulders are rigid. You need to relax, unwind, you won't enjoy this if you don't relax. What a waste, being here thinking about work! Just listen to the music and let it all go. Let the music do its work.
N: She'll be loving this.
She'll probably have forgotten I was late by now.
S: He'll be hating this.
N: Are they going to keep this up?

Harp Passage

S: *[Looks at her own hands]* Look at those hands.They're growing old. You've started to get old woman's hands. When did that happen?
N: Why is the harp Welsh? I wonder if she's Welsh.
S: That finger won't straighten properly anymore. I'd be no good up there. I bet they all have beautiful hands.
N: I'm not sure what the Welsh look like? Celtic look isn't it... does she look Celtic? Can't really see her behind that harp.
S: Maybe not... Maybe they have callouses. Do they have them insured? She has beautiful hands. I've got hands like my Mum.
N: *[Looking at S]* Why is she looking at her hands? Maybe she's bored. Perhaps I should have got her

that manicure instead. Thought this would be a good present – used to be able to judge these things. *[Sneeze]*

Bowed Strings Passage

S   *[Passing tissue]* He's got my cold. I suppose that's what we're going to share now, germs.

N   *[Looking at Harpist. Then the other players and finally the trombone player]* What do they think about when they're not playing?
That's the harpist thinking about now? Dreaming of the valleys?
What's he thinking? Car insurance, re-decorating, mortgage? Birthday present for the wife? What's she thinking? Berlin Philharmonic? New York? Her holidays?

S   *[Looking at Nick]* I wonder what he's thinking about? Not the music I bet. Then I'm not. Listen to the music, that's the whole point!

N: Who's up next then? Should be able to tell – who looks most tense? Trombone.

Marimba Passage

N: Damn… percussion!
How does he do that? How does he know how far apart to hold those beater things?

S: *[From Laurie Anderson's O Superman]*
Oh Johnny …. Oh Mum and Dad.
He looks like someone, Colin Farrell? Colin Firth.

Brass Passage

N: Hello, brass are back. At last. They barely play this lot. Hope they're not paid by the note, they'd starve. Wonder if the string players get more. He should be on time and a half the percussionist –

look at all that kit!
Supposed to be big drinkers the brass. Never see a woman in the brass section do you – in a brass band maybe – wonder if any of these started in a brass band? I think so, I can see them with peaked caps and shiny buttons, marching through the streets. I wonder how they got to be here?

String And Wind Passage

S: Snow, ice, icicles, frozen lake, cracking. Water, water droplets, water on a leaf in the sun. Sunny, birds, park, kids playing, shouting, summer.
N: She'll ask me questions later about my favourite bit.

Vibes Chords Passage

S: That was a beautiful change.
N: That might be my favourite bit.
This is a quiet bit.
[Looking down his row] Everyone's very quiet. Oh no, I think I've left my phone on.
[Looks for his phone] Oh no!
It's probably okay, it's Monday night, who's going to call? Nobody's going to call. Geoff, Geoff might call! Oh no he's bound to, "Do you want a pint mate?" "Not now, I'm in a concert!"
Where is it?

Low String And Brass Passage

N: *[Still looking for phone]* Where did I put it? Not in my trousers…
S: *[Looking at N]* What the hell's he up to now? Can't sit still for a minute. What's he …
N: Jacket, jacket. If I'm subtle no-one will notice.
S: He's getting his phone out! Surely he's not texting

Geoff? He's made this nice gesture and now he's ruining it!

High Strings Passage

S: He hasn't changed, in some ways that's a good thing. He's going grey, suits him though.

N: I wonder if she wishes I was more like one of them – like the percussionist – he looks pretty cool, got all that stuff. He's talented. It would be a different life. I'd be on tour a lot, be more interesting though. She could come with me, hang out with all of them, she could be friends with the flute player. They could talk about music. She'd love it.

S: I know Nicola thinks he's good looking.

N: Probably too late to learn an instrument now though.

S: We've still got things in common.

N: I hope she doesn't wish I was more like him.

Harp Passage

S: I like her shoes. That's a good choice, practical but smart, I wonder where she got them? Clarks probably.

N: If she was more like her I might be jealous – doing what she loves.

S: I should have dressed up a bit, made more of an effort.

N: All these people coming to see her. Admiring her.

S: Why's he wearing that shirt? I thought I threw it away!

Low Wind Passage

N: *[Trying to anticipate the notes]* Parp... Parp... Parp... Parp...

S: *[Looking at N]* What's he doing? He's moving his lips. He's like a mad old man.

N: "Once upon a time, there was an elephant, called Doris. She lived in the jungle. She was big and old and slow and grey…"

High Wind And Brass Passage

S: This is like that film.
N: What is that film?
S: Speeded up cars … you just see the trails of the lights.
N: Shots of deserts.
S: In America.
N: All over the world. We've got it at home
S: We've got it at home.

Glockenspiel Passage

S: I wonder if they lose track of the fact that we're here? Perhaps they've completely forgotten that we're here.
N: Violinist is looking at me, is she? She's definitely looking at me, why's she chosen me? Likes my shirt maybe?

Double Bass And Harp Passage

S: This is making me feel a bit tearful, making me feel a bit emotional. That's odd. I didn't think I was unhappy. Mind you, I did hear that bloke on the radio claiming that dissonance is a mild form of physical pain.

Ensemble Passage

Low Wind And Bass Passage

S: Well we didn't see that coming!
[Looking at N who is looking at the ceiling]

N: He's doing that film thing in his head. Bet he's doing a spy film in his head. He's so predictable and childish – he thinks that's what I like about him. Harry was walking alongside the river. Fog. Figure in the street light. Was that him? He couldn't be sure. The border guards shifted the weight of their rifles on their shoulders. He'd have to keep the drop discreet or the game would be up.

Low Strings Passage.

S: Are any of them lovers? I don't know. Him and her possibly? No, her and him, that's more likely. Or him and him? Maybe just the once, on tour, post show drinks, hotel corridor, bet it's rife.
N: Bitter. Bitter. Red wine. Red wine. White wine. Orange juice. Lager, foreign – Pils. Bloody Mary. Red wine. He looks like he's fond of it whatever it is.
S: If I had to, I'd go for the conductor. He looks very young. *[Looks through the programme]* born '72. 100 minus 72, 28 add 10… 38. He doesn't look 38. Nice arse.

Pizzicato Passage

N: This is great.
S: *[Quoting Desperate Housewives]* "And so this is how we learn that lovers aren't always more exciting than husbands".
N: I wish this bit could go on forever.
S: This bit's going down very well with our row.
N: I wonder if she's thinking about me at the same time as I'm thinking about her or if she's just thinking about the music?

Vibraphone Passage.

S: Why doesn't he talk to me more? Do we really like each other any more? If he does like me he doesn't show it. Where's the affection gone?

N: Maybe I should put my arm around her. Can you do that here? You can do it in the cinema. I'd like to... *[Looks around]*

S: Perhaps he's bored of me. I don't blame him. I'm bored of myself. Our lives are boring. We should do more of this. Bet he's bored.

N: I'm not sure this is romantic music but I'll do it. I will, I'll do it. No, it'll distract her, spoil it for her. I don't want to piss her off.

S: What if he wants to end it and just can't work out how to say so?

Strings And Bassoon Passage

S: I wonder if anyone else here is thinking thoughts like me? Bet everyone else is just listening to the music appreciating it. Is anyone else feeling like me here?

N: I think its worth isn't it, £14 a ticket? That's good value I think. How many are there? Quid per player and a couple for the conductor. I can't see how that covers it – this lot won't come cheap. Wonder how much they get? More than a teacher I bet, maybe not, no idea really.
Make the most of this now. This is great.

S: This is great.

Brass Passage

Bell Passage

S: This has got to be the last section, it's got that sense to it. We've not heard them before, they're on their own. The last clang echoes into the distance, a brief silence and then the applause and dash to be first to the loos. Come on, come on. Oh no! End. End. End.

Low Strings Passage.

S: Oh no, there's more!

Third Movement

[As each player takes their solo a short extract of an interview with them is heard. Through this material the audience learn a little about their lives or their playing or what they think about during performances]

Instrument **Topic**

Instrument	Topic
Harp:	Nervous.
Viola:	Love playing.
Percussion:	I could do better myself.
Double Bass:	CBSO 37 years.
Bassoon:	Found bassoon.
Trumpet:	Saliva.
Cello:	Practice not a chore.
Trombone:	Missing kids.
Double Bass:	Concentration and coffee.
Viola:	Wish I played something else.
Bass Clarinet:	Parents live in Scotland.
Violin:	Pilates.
Percussion:	No rules for downbeat.
Horn:	Wanted to play clarinet.
Flute:	Front teeth.
Harp:	French music.
Trumpet:	Food.
Flute:	Canals and curry.
Horn:	Pilot.
Cello:	How it works out.
Horn:	Good days and bad days.
Cello:	Listening and listening.

Harp:	Loading into car.
Bassoon:	Anything to do with music.
Flute:	Express yourself through music.
Trumpet:	Black shirt.
Bassoon:	Bass notes all day long.
Trumpet:	Real ale.
Viola:	Can't think about other things.
Bassoon:	Factory for parts.
Clarinet:	–
Cello:	Like to play bass clarinet.
Violin:	Looking at the audience.
Horn:	Tour manager.
Bassoon:	Practice gym.
Horn:	Conductor.
Viola:	Laughter.
Trumpet:	High wire act.
Viola:	Favourite piece.
Trumpet:	Designer black shirt.

During The Next Item In The Programme

N: *[Shortly into the first passage]* Koyaanisqatsi!

Original Programme Notes

"Going to a concert is always better than we expect it to be. We don't go often enough. The music is always better live than on the CD and there's always so much more going on than the music. The BCMG players are looking beautiful tonight and are under the no-nonsense baton of Richard Baker, so please, don't be late!" Stan's Cafe

Performed by:
Marie-Christine Zupancic, Jillian Allan, Margaret Cookhorn, Mark Philips, Jonathan Holland, Anthony Howe, Julian Warburton, Celine Saout, Alexandra Wood, Christopher Yates, Ulrich Heinen, John Tattersdill

Text devised and performed by:
Amanda Hadingue and Craig Stephens

Acting by Sarah Dawson and Nick Walker

Concept and direction: James Yarker
Composed by: Michael Wolters
Conducted by: Richard Baker

BCMG Artistic Director: Stephen Newbould
BCMG General Manager: Jackie Newbould
BCMG Marketing Manager: Tim Rushby
BCMG Learning Manager: Nancy Evans

Stan's Cafe General Manager: Charlotte Martin
Stan's Cafe Advisory Producer: Nick Sweeting

Thanks to: Everyone at MAC & the Sound Investors.

The Voyage

Eleven recorder players and a double bassist are arrayed far upstage. In front of a conductor. They are all in formal concert dress with laurel leaves on their heads. On a raised platform centre stage is Singer. She sings all the opera's text except where specified. All text except her's is spoken.

Performing in front of the musicians are a cast of actors who who lip synch with the singer when her words belong to their characters.

The audience sit on a raked seating bank facing the action. Unknown to them the seating bank is on wheels. At a point specified in the script the seating bank is moved steadily back away from the musicians and most of the actors. Approaching the opera's conclusion the seating bank moves rapidly back to its original position.

Announcement: (Part 1: 2'00")

The Voyage   *[Title Sign is raised]*
The Voyage
THE VOYAGE

Shh/he will be a hero   *[Rochi is introduced]*
After The Voyage
Now shh/he is nothing   *[Rochi always adds 'Shh'*
Then shh/he will be someone   *to her pronoun]*
After The Voyage

Packing Aria

[Mother arrives]
[Packing of suitcase]

Have you packed your lance? Do you have your spear?
Have you packed your jeans? Do you have your pants?
How about your hammer? Have you got your spikes?
Show me your raincoat. Where in there's your toothbrush?
Have you packed your shield? Do you have your helmet?
Have got your passport? Have you had your jabs?
How ab/

Rochi: Shhh

Farewell Duet: (Part 2: 7'00")

<u>Mother.</u>	<u>Son.</u>
So young	So ready
I don't want you to go	I must go, you know
	It's all I've ever wanted
All you've ever worked for	All I've ever worked for
All you've ever wanted	
	It's the one thing I'm good for
It's all you've ever dreamed of	Today I am just no-body
Tomorrow you'll be golden	

I love you	I know
I'll miss you	You won't
I will	It's not long
It's far	I'm ready
Be safe	I'll try
Be fast	I will

You will be strong
You will be brave
You will be pure
You will be true
You will be fast fast fast fast FAST!

[Athlete climbs onto a plank jutting from the front of the seating bank. The seating bank retreats]

Sail far
Sail fair
Sail clear
Sail straight
Good luck
Come back
I love you

Commentary for the Journey

He was tempted   [Manager arrives]
He was tainted
He was vaunted   [Journalist arrives]
He was feted   [Photographer arrives]
And he ran

He was washed up
He was wound up   [Hoodies 1 & 2 arrive]
He was held up
He was messed up
And he ran

He came from over the seas
He was picked up and adopted   [Father arrives]
He was a Cared For Child
He had a child   [Girlfriend arrives]
And he ran

He was spotted   [Athletics Man arrives]
He was coached   [Coach arrives]
He was hugged
He was picked   [Training Partner arrives]

And he ran

And he laughed and he stretched and he lifted and he fasted.
And he chased and he wretched and he pressed and squatted.
And he did all the things they ever asked him to.
Until in the end they called him theirs.

He was a monk
He was a warrior
He was a woah/man   [Rochi adds 'woah']
And he ran and he ran and he ran UNTIL.

The Get Set

[The seating bank stops and blue fabric sea is removed to reveal a running track]

Athlete: The time for running had to stop.
           Her time had come.
           She had to face the crowd.
           She had to knuckle down.

57

Conductor: Marks

Athlete: The cheering falls silent.
The crowd stop breathing.
A single bird flies overhead.   *[Mechanical bird]*
Everyone leans in.

Conductor: Set

Athlete: Nothing but the white line tunnel.
A shot.

Conductor: GO!

The Race

*[The Athlete starts running, the seating bank follows.
The Athlete falls and her Mother runs to comfort her.
The seating bank travels over both Athlete and Mother.]*

[A new Athlete - one of the hoodies - has appeared and in slow motion crosses the line to be welcomed in rapture by everyone who had previously been attached to our heroic athlete]

So it is and
So it is
People
Now hail your champion
All hail your great bright hero
He fought the lion and he slew the dragon
He sailed through storms, defeated the waves.
All hail our champion
Once he was a dwarf, now he is a giant
Soon free to air
Now you can kiss me, come to my cloud.

[The winner has climbed up beside the singer who crowns her with laurels]

Credits

Mezzo-soprano: Suzanna Purkis
Recorder: Michelle Holloway
Recorder: Kathryn Bennetts
Recorder: Peter Bowman
Double Bass: Sebastiano Dessanay
Ensemble recorders:
Sarah Langdon, Clare Murphy, Kate Rose, Charlotte Hiller,
Ben Rose, Maryanne Coughlan, Kathryn Harris, Emily Bannister
Conductor: Dan Watson

Athlete: Rochi Rampal: Athlete
Mother: Janet Behan: Mother
Girlfriend: Alice Greenham: Girlfriend
Hoodie #1 / Winner: Danni Leppier
Hoodie #2: Luke Bowes
Manager: Gerard Bell
Coach: Adele Fowles
Journalist: Craig Stephens
Photographer: Graeme Rose
Atlas #1 & Atlas #2: Ian & Jim Wyatt-Lees

Music: Michael Wolters
Libretto: James Yarker
Direction: Craig Stephens & James Yarker
Set Design & Stage Management: Harry Trow
Seating Bank Design & Construction: Adrian Bradley
Lighting: Mick Diver
Secret Atlases: Mic & Josh Mac
General Manager: Charlotte Martin

New Music 20x12 is a UK-wide commissioning programme initiated by Jillian Barker and David Cohen, and delivered by PRS for Music Foundation in partnership with the BBC, LOCOG, Sound and Music and NMC Recordings.

New Music 20x12 is generously supported by the following committed patrons and funders: Arts Council England, Creative Scotland, John S. Cohen Foundation, PRS for Music Foundation, Arts Council of Northern Ireland, Arts Council of Wales, Columbia Foundation Fund of the Capital Community Foundation, Incorporated Society of Musicians, Musicians Benevolent Fund, Jerwood Charitable Foundation, RVW Trust, Charlotte and Dennis Stevenson, Tolkien Trust, The Leche Trust, The Bliss Trust, Finzi Trust, The Worshipful Company of Musicians, Lilian Slowe, John and Ann Tusa, John Wates Charitable Trust, Richard Walduck, Honeymead Arts Trust, and Sir Anthony Cleaver.

New Music 20x12 is a UK wide programme which consists of twenty outstanding new works, each lasting 12 minutes, commissioned to feature centre stage of the London 2012 Cultural Olympiad. New Music 20x12 commissions will be broadcast by BBC Radio 3 and tour the UK, enabling as many people as possible to enjoy excellent new music as part of our celebrations of the London 2012 Olympic Games and Paralympic Games.

About the illustration and design

The illustrations for the covers of these books were undertaken by students at Birmingham City University as the final module of their first-year illustration course during the Spring/Summer of 2018. The images were developed using workshops using variations of the theatre-devising methods produced by Stan's Cafe but adapted and applied to the making of visual work. The resulting work was shown in the pop-up exhibition *The Something Of Somebody Something* at AE Harris in May 2018.

The design concept of the books was produced by final year Graphic Design student Aimee Chapman. These were then further developed for print in a collaborative process between Stan's Cafe and the University's Innovation Product Support Service (IPSS) and involved helping the company with selecting appropriate DTP software, undertaking training and selecting a suitable print on demand service.

Gareth Courage
Lecturer in Illustration
Birmingham City University

www.ingramcontent.com/pod-product-compliance
Lightning Source LLC
Chambersburg PA
CBHW071756080526
44588CB00013B/2260